Gallaudet
Survival Guide to
Signing

Gallaudet
Survival Guide to
Signing

LEONARD G. LANE

Illustrations by
JAN SKROBISZ

Gallaudet University Press
Washington, D.C.

For my loving and supportive family

First Edition, 1987

Gallaudet University Press, Washington, DC 20002
© 1990, 1987 by Gallaudet University. All rights reserved
Published 1990
Second Printing, 1990. Third printing, 1993
Printed in the United States of America

Library of Congress Cataloging-in-Publication Data
Lane, Leonard G.
  Gallaudet survival guide to signing / Leonard G. Lane ;
illustrations by Jan Skrobisz.
    p.   cm.
  ISBN 0-930323-67-X : $4.95
  1. Sign language—Dictionaries. I. Skrobisz, Jan. II. Title.
HV2475.L36 1990
419'.03—dc20   89-25686
                                                    CIP

Contents

Foreword

Since my appointment as the first deaf president of Gallaudet University, I have witnessed firsthand a great surge of interest in deafness and deaf people here in the United States and abroad. We at Gallaudet University appreciate very much this new awareness and sensitivity to deafness as an indication that the unnecessary communication gap that has existed for too long between deaf and hearing people is narrowing. This book is another contribution to closing that gap.

The first edition of the *Gallaudet Survival Guide to Signing* sold more than 85,000 copies! Not only has this handy little book helped many people learn basic signs, it also has introduced them to deafness and deaf people. The experience will open up a fascinating new world. It can enrich your life and whet your appetite to learn more about the beauty of sign language, the richness of deaf culture, and the proud heritage of deaf people and the deaf community.

The *Survival Guide* is an excellent resource for parents of deaf children and those with deaf friends, classmates, relatives, neighbors, and co-workers because it provides them with a natural, comfortable means of communication. The book's basic sign vocabulary also could be of critical use to safety and medical professionals coping with emergency situations involving deaf people.

By bringing deaf and hearing people closer together, we can improve the world for all of us. The *Gallaudet Survival Guide to Signing* is another step toward that goal.

I. King Jordan
President
Gallaudet University

Introduction

Since you picked up this book, you probably want to learn sign language . . . good for you! Sign language is a beautiful, visually expressive language. People who use sign language will appreciate your efforts to learn to communicate with them.

The *Survival Guide* is an easy reference you can carry with you. It has more than 500 signs for use in home, school, work, or social situations. Of course, there are hundreds more signs besides the ones in this book. But once you have learned the sign/words in the *Survival Guide,* you will be well on your way to communicating in sign language.

When you are just beginning to learn sign language, you may feel frustrated because you won't know many signs. Don't worry—when you don't know the sign for a word or concept, you can always fingerspell it. Fingerspelling allows you to spell each letter of a word by using your hand to form each of the 26 letters of the alphabet. These handshapes, known as the American Manual Alphabet, are on pages viii and ix. As you learn more and more signs, you will find that some words or concepts don't have a sign equivalent, so you will always have a use for fingerspelling.

American Sign Language (ASL) is the major sign system used by deaf people in the United States. It is a language of its own, with its own grammar rules, including different word order rules than English has. Signs represent specific concepts just as words do in spoken languages. As a beginning signer, you can use ASL signs in the same order as you would words in an English sentence. Using ASL signs in this way is known as pidgin signing. Most deaf people will understand you when you use this form of signing.

Hints for Using This Book

To help you learn the signs in this book, a written description of how to form each sign accompanies each sign illustration. The arrows indicate the direction your hand(s) move in forming the sign. If a sign has more than one part, the first position is drawn lighter than the second position.

The capital letters used to describe handshapes (for example, A shape, B shape, etc.) refer to the manual alphabet handshapes (see pp. viii–ix). The numbers describing handshapes (for example, ONE shape, 5 shape, 9 shape, etc.) refer to the manual number handshapes (see p. x). Some modified or special handshapes are used frequently in signing; these are on page vii. *Palm in* means the palm of the hand should be facing the body while *palm out* means the palm should be facing away from the body.

Occasionally, you will see a note in a sign description that the sign can be *initialized*. This means that you can use the manual alphabet handshape for the first letter of the word you are signing. For example, the sign for *am* can be made two ways—with the index finger extended and pointing up or with the letter A handshape making the same movement.

The signers in this book are right handed. If you are left handed, reverse the signs as they are shown. *The sign illustrations are drawn as they would be seen by the viewer, not the signer.* Practicing in front of the mirror will enable you to see your signs as they look in this book and as they will look to the person reading your signs.

Suggestions for Effective Signing

1. Practice so that your signing becomes smooth and clear.
2. Increase your speed as you become more familiar with signs.
3. Don't try to sign fast. Pace your signing to synchronize with your speech.
4. As a general rule, make your signs in the area between the top of your head and waist and between your shoulders.
5. Keep your hand steady when you fingerspell. Find a comfortable position, about mid-chest level, for your hand.
6. Use good facial expressions and body language as you sign to help others understand what you are communicating.
7. Practice, practice, practice—alone and with others, especially with your deaf co-worker, relative, friend, or neighbor. It is the best way to learn signs and become a good signer.

Special Handshapes

AND shape

curved 5 shape

CLAW shape

bent V shape

open and bent hand

American Manual Alphabet

A

B

C

D

E

F

G

H

I

J

K

L

M N O P

Q R S T

U V W X

Y Z

Manual Numbers

0

1

2

3

4

5

6

7

8

9

10

11

12

13

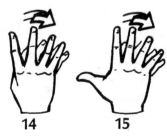

14

15

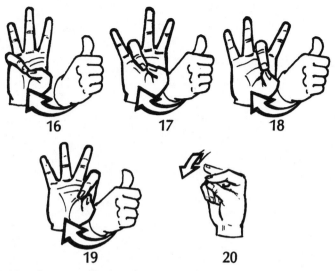

16   17   18

19   20

Numbers can be used in many different situations for a variety of purposes. Some of the ways you can use numbers are explained below.

Addresses   Sign the numbers in the order you speak them, then fingerspell the name of the street. For example: 5152 Arctic Avenue is signed as 51, 52 a-r-c-t-i-c. a-v-e.

Time   Sign the numbers in the order you speak them. For example, you can tell someone it is 4:15 by signing 4, 15.

Dates   Sign the numbers in the order you speak them. For example, 1776 is signed as 17, 7, 6.

Money   Sign the amount in numbers and then the sign for *dollar*. For example, $14 is signed as 14 + *dollar*.

Gallaudet
Survival Guide to
Signing

A a

about

Right hand in ONE shape, palm in, index finger pointing left. Left hand in AND shape, palm in, fingers pointing right. Move right index finger around left fingertips.

above, over

Both hands open, palms down, right fingers pointing left, left fingers pointing right. Place right palm on back of left hand. Move right hand up and around toward body.

accept

Both hands in curved 5 shape in front of chest, palms down, fingers pointing out. Close hands to AND shape while moving them in against chest.

accident

Both hands in curved 5 shape in front of shoulders, palms in. Move hands together while closing to S shape, ending with knuckles touching in front of chest.

ache, hurt

Both hands in ONE shape, palms in, right index finger pointing left, left index finger pointing right. With hands in front of chest, move index fingers toward each other several times without touching.

across

Both hands open, right palm facing left, fingers pointing out; left palm down, fingers pointing right. Put left hand in front of right hand. Then move right hand over left hand in an arc.

act, do

Both hands in C shape in front of waist, palms down. Move hands back and forth from left to right several times.

add

Left hand in AND shape in front of chest, palm in, fingers pointing right. Right hand in curved 5 shape below left hand, palm down, fingers pointing out. Move right hand up while closing to AND shape, ending with hands touching.

address

Both hands in 10 shape, palms in, thumbs up. Move hands up sides of chest.

afraid

Both hands in S shape at sides of chest, palms in. Move hands up to center of chest, ending with hands open.

after (time)

Both hands open in front of chest, palms in, right fingers pointing left, left fingers pointing right. Place palm of right hand against back of left hand. Then move right hand out and away from left hand.

afternoon

Right arm extended outward, hand open, palm down. Left arm across chest, palm down, fingers pointing right. Rest right arm on back of left hand. Then lower right palm slightly and repeat.

again

Right hand open and bent, palm up. Left hand open, palm up, fingers pointing out. Turn right hand over and down, touching fingertips against left palm.

agree

Both hands in ONE shape, palms down, left index finger pointing out. Touch forehead with right index fingertip. Then bring right finger down, ending with both index fingers parallel.

airplane

Right thumb, index and little fingers extended, pointing out, hand above shoulder, palm down. Move hand forward a short distance and repeat.

alarm

Right hand in ONE shape, palm facing left, index finger pointing up. Left hand open, palm facing right, fingers pointing up. Tap right index finger quickly against left palm and repeat.

all

Right hand open and flat near shoulder, palm out, fingers pointing left. Left hand open and flat at an angle in front of chest. Move right hand to right and out in an arc, ending with back of right hand in left palm.

allow, let, way

Both hands open in front of waist, palms facing, fingers pointing out. Move hands out and slightly up.

almost

Both hands open, palms up. Place fingers of right hand under fingertips of left hand and brush upward.

am (all forms of *be*)

Right hand in ONE shape, palm facing left. Place index fingertip at lips. Then move finger out in short, straight line. (Note: This sign can be initialized by using the A shape.)

America

Both hands in 5 shape, palms facing at an angle, fingers pointing out. Interlock fingers of both hands. Then move hands out and around in circle in front of chest.

among

Right hand in ONE shape. Left hand in 5 shape in front of chest, palm in. Move right index finger in and out between fingers of left hand beginning at little finger.

and

Right hand in curved 5 shape, fingers pointing left. Move hand from left to right in front of chest while closing tips of fingers and thumb.

angry, mad

Right hand in 5 shape, palm in, fingers pointing up. Place hand in front of face. Then bend fingers, ending in CLAW shape.

announce

Both hands in ONE shape, palms in, index fingers touching chin. Move hands out and to sides, ending with palms out and index fingers pointing up.

another, other

Right hand in 10 shape, palm down. Move hand up and to right, ending with palm up.

answer

Both hands in ONE shape, palms out, right hand under lips, left hand slightly in front of right hand. Move hands down, ending with index fingers pointing out.

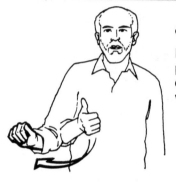

any

Right hand in 10 shape, palm facing left. Move hand down and to right, ending with palm down.

apple

Right hand in X shape, palm out. Press knuckle of index finger on right cheek and twist.

appointment

Both hands in A shape, right hand with bent wrist in front of right shoulder, left hand in front of waist, palm down. Circle right hand out and around, ending with right wrist against side of left hand.

are (all forms of *be*)

Right hand in ONE shape, palm facing left. Place index fingertip at lips. Then move finger out in short, straight line. (Note: This sign can be initialized by using the R shape.)

area

Both hands in A shape in front of chest, palms down, thumbs almost touching. Circle hands out and around toward body, ending with thumbs touching.

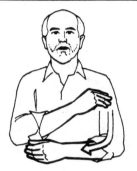

arm

Right hand open and bent, palm down. Left hand open, palm in, arm bent. Move right hand down left arm.

around

Both hands in ONE shape, palms in, right index finger pointing down, left index finger pointing up. With right hand above left hand, move right finger around left finger.

around

Right hand open in front of body, palm down. Move hand in counterclockwise circle.

arrange,
plan (verb),
schedule (verb)

Both hands open in front of
body, palms facing, fingers
pointing out. Move hands to
right.

arrive

Right hand open in front of
right shoulder, palm in,
fingers pointing up. Left hand
open in front of chest, palm
up, fingers pointing out.
Move right hand forward and
down, ending with back of
right hand on left palm.

ask (request)

Both hands open and apart
in front of chest, palms
facing, fingers pointing up.
Bring palms together.

ask (a question)

Right hand in D shape near right side of face. Move hand out and down, ending with index finger in X shape.

assist, help

Left hand open, palm up. Right hand in 10 shape, palm in, resting on left palm. Raise right hand with left hand.

attention

Both hands open at sides of face, palms facing, fingers pointing up. Move both hands forward and down.

 **Bb**

baby

Right hand open, palm up at an angle, fingers facing left. Left hand open, palm up, fingers pointing right. Put right hand on lower left arm. Then rock arms back and forth.

bad

Right hand in B shape, palm in, fingertips on lips. Move hand away and down while twisting wrist, ending with palm down.

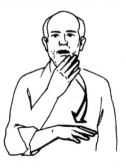

banana

Right thumb and index fingertips touching, other fingers closed. Left hand in ONE shape, palm in, index finger pointing up. Move tips of right thumb and finger down left index finger as if peeling a banana.

be (all forms of *be*)

Right hand in ONE shape, palm facing left. Place tip of finger at lips. Then move finger out in short, straight line. (Note: This sign can be initialized by using the B shape.)

beautiful

Right hand in 5 shape near right side of face, palm in, fingers pointing up. Move hand in circle in front of face while closing to AND shape, ending near chin. Then move hand out slightly while opening to 5 shape, palm in.

because

Right hand in L shape, palm in, index finger pointing left. Touch forehead with index fingertip. Then move hand up slightly to right, closing to 10 shape.

bed

Right hand open, palm facing left, fingers pointing up. Place hand against right side of face and tilt head slightly to right.

beer

Right hand in B shape, palm facing left, fingers pointing up. Put edge of right index finger near right side of mouth. Then draw hand down and repeat several times.

before (time)

Both hands open, palms in. Place back of right hand in left palm. Then move right hand in toward chest.

begin, start

Right hand in ONE shape, palm down, index finger pointing left. Left hand in 5 shape, palm facing right, fingers pointing out. Twist right index finger between left index and middle fingers.

behind

Both hands in A shape in front of chest, palms facing, thumbs up. Place hands together. Then move right hand in back of left hand.

believe

Right hand in ONE shape,
index finger touching right
temple. Left hand open in
front of chest, palm up.
Move right hand down while
opening and clasp left hand.

below (distance)

Both hands B shape, palms
down, right fingers pointing
left, left fingers pointing
right. Put back of right hand
under palm of left hand.
Then move right hand down
and inward in counter-
clockwise motion.

best

Right hand open, palm in,
fingers pointing left. Place
hand in front of mouth. Then
move hand up to right while
changing to 10 shape.

better

Right hand open in front of mouth, palm in, fingers pointing left. Move hand to right while changing to 10 shape.

between

Both hands open, right palm facing left, fingers pointing out; left palm in, fingers pointing right. Put right little finger on left index finger and move back and forth between left thumb and index fingertip.

big, large

Both hands in curved L shape in front of chest, palms in at an angle. Move hands out, ending with palms facing out.

bird

Right hand in G shape at mouth, palm down, thumb and index fingers pointing out. Open and close thumb and index finger several times.

birthday

Right hand open on chest, palm in, fingers pointing left. Left hand open in front of waist, palm up, fingers pointing out. Move right hand out and down, ending with back of right hand on left palm.

black

Right hand in ONE shape, palm down. Draw finger across forehead above eyebrows from left to right.

blame

Right hand in 10 shape, palm facing left. Left hand in A shape, palm down. Brush right hand across back of left hand and repeat.

blouse

Both hands open and slightly curved at sides of chest, palms in at an angle. Move hands out and down, ending with hands at waist.

blue

Right hand in B shape, palm facing left, fingers pointing up. Wave hand back and forth by twisting wrist.

body

Both hands open, palms in, fingertips facing. Place hands on upper chest. Then move them down and place them on lower chest.

book

Both hands open in front of chest, palms together, fingers pointing out. Open hands at top, keeping little fingers together.

born

Both hands open in front of chest, palms in, right fingers pointing left, left fingers pointing right. Place back of right hand against left palm. Then move right hand down and out to right, ending with palm down.

borrow

Both hands in K shape in front of lower chest, fingers pointing out. Put little finger side of right K hand on index finger side of left K hand. Then move fingers up and in toward upper chest, ending with fingers pointing up.

both

Right hand in V shape, palm in, fingers pointing up. Left hand curved, palm in, fingers pointing right. Place right wrist in left palm. Then while closing left hand, move right hand down, changing from V to U shape.

bother

Right hand open, fingers together, thumb up, palm facing left. Left hand in flat C shape, palm in. Move little finger side of right hand into notch between left thumb and index finger twice.

box (noun)

Both hands open in front of
body, left hand in front of
right hand, palms in. Move
hands to sides of body,
ending with palms facing
and fingers pointing out.

boy

Right hand in flat C shape
above right eye. Close thumb
and fingertips several times.

bread

Both hands open and bent
slightly, left palm in, fingers
pointing right. Draw right
fingertips down back of left
fingers several times.

break

Both hands in S shape side by side in front of chest, palms down. Move hands apart quickly with outward twist, ending with palms up.

breakfast

Right hand in AND shape. Touch lips with fingertips twice. Then lower and extend right arm, palm up. Put fingertips of left hand in crook of slightly bent right arm. Move open right hand upward.

bright, clear, light

Both hands in AND shape in front of chest, palms out. Move hands up and away from each other, opening to 5 shape, palms out.

bring

Both hands open, palms up in front of waist, fingers pointing out. Move hands in an arc from right to left.

brother

Left hand in L shape in front of waist, thumb up, index finger pointing out. Place right hand in 10 shape above right eye. Then bring right hand down while changing to L shape, ending with right hand resting on left hand.

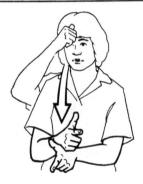

brown

Right hand in B shape, palm out, fingers pointing up. Rub edge of index finger down right cheek and repeat.

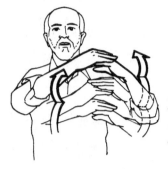

build, building

Both hands open and bent, palms down, right fingers pointing left, left fingers pointing right. Overlap fingers while moving hands up and over each other alternately.

business

Right hand in B shape, palm out, fingers pointing up. Left hand in B shape, palm down. Strike right wrist against left wrist several times.

busy

Right hand in B shape, palm out, fingers pointing up. Left hand in B shape, palm down. Put right wrist against side of left hand. Move right hand slightly from side to side.

but, different

Both hands in ONE shape, palms out. Cross index fingers and then draw them apart.

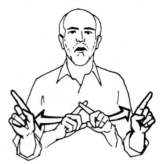

butter

Right hand in U shape. Left hand open, palm up, fingers pointing out. Draw fingertips of right U across left palm twice.

buy

Right hand in AND shape, palm up. Left hand open, palm up, fingers pointing out. Place back of right fingers on left palm. Then lift right hand up and move it forward slightly.

C c

cake

Right hand in C shape, palm down. Left hand open, palm up. Place right fingertips in left palm. Then move right hand out across left palm and repeat.

can (verb)

Both hands in A shape side by side in front of chest, palms down. Move hands down firmly.

cancel

Right hand in ONE shape.
Left hand open, palm up,
fingers pointing out at an
angle. Draw an X with right
index fingertip on left palm.

candy

Right hand in U shape, palm
in. By bending fingers, rub
fingertips of right U down
chin several times.

can't

Both hands in ONE shape,
palms down. Bring right
index finger down, striking
left index fingertip in
passing.

car

Both hands in S shape, palms in. Move hands up and down at an angle alternately as if turning a steering wheel.

careful

Both hands in V shape, right palm facing left, left palm facing right. Cross wrists and strike together several times.

carry

Both hands open, palms up, fingers pointing out. Move hands in two movements from right to left in front of body.

cat

Right hand in F shape, palm facing left. Put hand at right side of mouth and move it out to right.

catch

Right hand in curved 5 shape at shoulder, palm out. Left hand in S shape in front of chest, palm right. Move right hand down, while closing to S shape, onto side of left hand.

center

Left hand open in front of chest, palm up, fingers pointing out. Right hand open, palm down, above left hand. Circle right hand over left hand. Then touch left palm with fingertips of right bent hand.

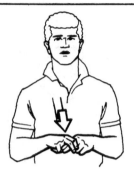

chair

Both hands in U shape, palms down. Tap curved right U fingers across back of left U fingers twice.

change (verb)

Both hands in A shape, palms facing. Place knuckles of hands together and twist in opposite directions.

charge

Right hand in X shape, palm in. Left hand open, palm facing right, fingers pointing out. Move right bent index finger down left palm.

check (noun)

Both hands in L shape in front of chin, palms out, tips of thumbs and index fingers touching. Move hands to sides with index fingers pointing up, ending with tips of thumbs and index fingers touching.

check (verb)

Right hand in ONE shape. Left hand open, palm up, fingers pointing out. Put right index finger near right eye. Then move it down to left palm and make a check mark off the palm.

cheese

Both hands open, right palm down, left palm up. Rub and twist heel of right hand on heel of left hand.

child

Right hand open at waist level, palm down, fingers pointing out. Move hand down slightly twice.

children

Right hand open in front of waist, palm down, fingers pointing out. Move hand out to right in short bouncing motions.

choice

Both hands in 5 shape in front of chest, palms facing, fingers pointing up. Bend right thumb and index finger and place them near left index finger. Then move right hand back while closing tips of thumb and index finger and repeat.

choose, pick, select

Bend thumb and index finger
of open right hand in front of
chest, palm out. Then draw
hand back while closing tips
of thumb and index finger.

city, town

Both hands open in front of
chest, palms facing at an
angle, fingertips touching.
Move hands apart and to the
right, ending with fingertips
touching.

class

Both hands in C shape in
front of chest, palms facing.
Circle hands out and around
until little fingers touch.

clean, nice

Both hands open, right palm down, left palm up. Place right palm on heel of left palm. Then move right hand across to left fingertips.

clear, bright, light

Both hands in AND shape in front of chest, palms out. Move hands up and away from each other, opening to 5 shape, palms out.

climb

Both hands in curved 5 shape in front of chest, left hand slightly higher than right hand, palms facing. Move right hand above left, then left hand above right and repeat.

clock

Right hand in ONE shape, palm down. Left hand in S shape, palm down. Tap left wrist with right index finger. Then move hands up in front of face, opening them into C shape with thumbs and fingers touching.

close

Both hands open near sides of body, palms up, fingers pointing out. Flip hands over, ending with index fingers touching and palms down.

clothes

Both hands in 5 shape near shoulders, palms in. Brush fingertips downward on chest several times.

coat

Both hands in 10 shape near shoulders, palms facing. Move hands downward in an arc to the waist.

coffee

Both hands in S shape, palms in. Place right hand on left hand and make circular motions with right hand.

cold (sickness)

Right hand in G shape. Put tips of thumb and index finger near nose. Then move hand down while closing tips of thumb and index finger and repeat.

cold, winter

Both hands in S shape at sides, palms facing. Move hands back and forth toward each other in short, shaking motions.

college

Both hands open, right palm down, left palm up, fingers pointing out at an angle. Place right palm on left palm. Then move right hand up and out in a circular motion.

color

Right hand in 5 shape, palm in, fingers pointing up. Wiggle fingertips in front of chin.

come

Both hands in ONE shape, palms up, index fingers pointing out. Bring index fingers up toward body in beckoning motion.

complain

Right hand in CLAW shape, palm in. Tap chest twice with fingertips.

control, direct, manage

Both hands in X shape in front of chest, palms facing, knuckles pointing out. Move hands in and out alternately.

cook

Both hands open, right palm down, fingers pointing left; left palm up, fingers pointing out. Place right palm on left palm. Then turn right hand over, placing back of hand on left palm. Repeat several times.

cookie

Right hand in CLAW shape, palm down. Left hand open, palm up. Put right fingertips on left palm. Then twist right hand back and forth several times.

correct (adjective), right (correct)

Both hands in ONE shape, palms facing, index fingers pointing out. Strike edge of right little finger on top of left index finger.

cost

Both hands in 9 shape in front of shoulders, palms out. Move hands back and forth toward each other, ending with hands together, thumbs touching.

count

Right hand in 9 shape, palm down. Left hand open, palm up, fingers pointing out. Move tips of right thumb and index finger along left palm from heel to fingertips.

cup

Right hand in C shape, palm facing left. Left hand open, palm up, fingers pointing right. Place edge of right little finger on left palm.

cut

Right hand in V shape, palm in, fingers pointing left. Make cutting motion with index and middle fingers while moving hand left across chest, ending in H shape.

cute, sugar

Right hand in H shape, thumb extended, palm in. Place tips of index and middle fingers on chin. Brush chin several times with fingertips, ending with hand in 10 shape below chin.

cut off

Right hand in V shape, palm facing left, fingers pointing out. Left hand open, palm down, fingers pointing right. Make cutting motion with right index and middle fingers, moving them across left fingertips.

Dd

daily, everyday, every day

Right hand in A shape, palm in. Rub knuckles of hand forward and back on right cheek several times.

dark

Both hands open in front of shoulders, palms in, fingers pointing up. Pass hands in front of face, moving them down and ending with hands crossed in front of chest.

daughter

Right hand in A shape, palm facing left. Left hand open in front of waist, palm up, fingers pointing right. Move right thumb along right cheek and chin and down to left arm, ending with open right hand, palm up, in crook of left arm.

day

Right hand in D shape, palm facing left, index finger pointing up. Left hand in front of waist, palm down, fingers pointing right. Place right elbow on back of left hand. Then lower right arm, ending with right index finger on left elbow.

deaf

Right hand in ONE shape, palm facing left. First touch right ear with index fingertip. Then move fingertip down to right corner of mouth.

deaf

Right hand in ONE shape, palm facing left. Left hand in B shape at left side, palm at an angle. First touch right ear with right index fingertip. Then while changing right hand to B shape, move both hands down in front of waist, ending with index fingers touching.

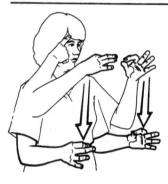

decide

Right hand in ONE shape, palm in. First touch right forehead with right index fingertip. Then with both hands in F shape in front of shoulders, drop hands to waist level.

department

Both hands in D shape in front of chest, palms facing, index fingers pointing up. Move hands out and around in a circular motion until little fingers touch.

desk, table

Both hands open, palms
down, right fingers pointing
left, left fingers pointing
right. Move right forearm
and hand down and place
on top of left forearm and
hand; tap twice.

dictionary

Right hand in D shape, palm
down. Left hand open, palm
up, fingers pointing out.
Move right hand in circular
motion across left palm.

different, but

Both hands in ONE shape,
palms down. Cross index
fingers. Then pull hands
apart.

difficult, hard (difficult)

Both hands in bent V shape, palms in. Move hands up and down alternately, striking knuckles together as they pass.

dinner

Right hand in D shape near right side of mouth, palm in. Move hand in, touching face with thumb and middle fingertips and repeat.

direct, control, manage

Both hands in X shape in front of chest, palms facing, knuckles pointing out. Move hands in and out alternately.

dirt, dirty

Right hand in 5 shape, palm down, fingers pointing left. Place back of right hand under chin and wiggle fingers.

disappoint, miss (feel lack of)

Right hand in ONE shape, palm in. Touch chin with index fingertip.

discuss

Right hand in ONE shape, palm facing in, index finger pointing out. Left hand open, palm up, fingers pointing out at an angle. Strike side of right index finger against left palm several times.

doctor

Right hand in M shape, palm down. Left hand open, palm up, fingers pointing out. Place fingertips of right M on left wrist. (Note: This sign can be initialized by using right hand in the D shape.)

dog

Right hand in front of waist, palm up. Snap thumb and middle fingers together twice.

dollar

Left hand open, palm in, fingers pointing right. Bend right hand, palm down, over left index finger. Then move right hand from left thumb out and off left fingertips.

don't, not

Right hand in 10 shape, palm facing left. Put tip of thumb under chin and move hand outward.

don't know

Right hand open at right side of head, palm facing in, fingers pointing left. Move hand down and out, ending with palm out, fingers pointing up.

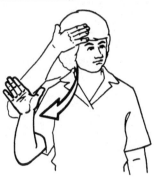

don't like

Right hand in 8 shape, palm in. Place tips of thumb and middle finger on chest. Move hand out and to right, ending with hand open, palm down.

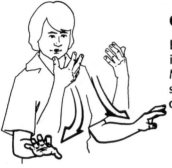

don't want

Both hands in CLAW shape in front of chest, palms up. Move hands down and out to sides, ending with palms down.

door

Both hands in B shape side by side, palms out, index fingers touching. Swing right hand back until palm faces left and repeat.

down

Right hand in ONE shape, palm in, index finger pointing down. Move finger down.

draw

Right hand in I shape. Left
hand open, palm in at an
angle. Move right little finger
across left palm in wiggling
motion.

dress (verb)

Both hands in 5 shape near
shoulders, palms in. Brush
fingertips downward on
chest.

drink

Right hand in C shape
slightly below chin, palm
facing left. Move hand up,
tipping it toward mouth as if
drinking.

drive

Both hands in S shape in front of shoulders, palms in. Move hands outward.

drop

Both hands in S shape in front of chest, palms down. Drop and open hands suddenly.

dry

Right hand in X shape, palm down. Draw bent index finger left to right across chin.

Ee

each, every

Both hands in A shape, right palm facing left, left palm facing right. Draw right knuckles down left thumb and repeat.

ear

Hold earlobe between thumb and index finger of right hand and shake.

early

Right hand in 5 shape, palm down, middle finger bent. Left hand open, palm down, fingers pointing right. Move right middle finger outward across back of left hand.

easy

Both hands open and bent slightly, palms up. Brush back of left fingers with right fingers several times.

eat, food

Right hand in AND shape. Touch lips with fingertips several times.

egg

Both hands in H shape, palms facing at an angle. Strike left index finger with right middle finger, then quickly drop hands down and apart.

either, or, then

Right hand in ONE shape. Left hand in L shape, palm facing right, index finger pointing out. With right index finger, first touch left thumb, then left index finger.

electric, electricity

Both hands in X shape, palms in. Strike knuckles of bent index fingers together several times.

elevator

Right hand in E shape, palm out. Left hand open, palm out at an angle, fingers pointing up. Move right hand up and down left palm.

empty

Right hand in 5 shape, palm down, middle finger bent. Left hand open, palm down, fingers pointing right. Move right middle finger along back of left hand and lift off fingertips.

end

Both hands in B shape, crossed, little finger side of right hand on index finger side of left hand. Move right hand along left index finger, dropping right hand off left fingertips.

enjoy

Both hands open, palms in, right fingers pointing left, left fingers pointing right. Place right hand above left hand on chest and move hands in opposite circular motions. (Note: This sign can be done with only one hand.)

enough

Right hand open, palm down, fingers pointing out at an angle. Left hand in S shape, palm facing right. Brush right palm outward across left index finger and thumb and repeat.

evening

Right hand open and bent, palm down, fingers pointing out. Left hand open, palm down, fingers pointing right. Tap right wrist against back of left hand.

every, each

Both hands in A shape, right palm facing left, left palm facing right. Draw right knuckles down left thumb and repeat.

everyday, every day, daily

Right hand in A shape, palm in. Rub knuckles of hand forward and back on right cheek several times.

example, show (verb)

Right hand in ONE shape, palm in. Left hand open, palm out, fingers pointing up. Place right index fingertip on left palm. Then move both hands forward. (Note: This sign can be initialized by using the right hand in the E shape.)

excuse me

Right hand open and bent, palm down. Left hand open, palm up. Brush right fingertips outward across left fingertips and repeat.

explain

Both hands in F shape in front of body, palms facing, fingers pointing out. Move hands in and out alternately.

eye

Right hand in ONE shape. Point to right eye. (Note: For eyes, point first to right eye, then to left one.)

F f

face

Right hand in ONE shape.
Trace a circle around the
face.

fall (season)

Right hand in 4 shape, palm
down. Left arm bent, hand in
S shape near chin, palm
facing right. Brush side of
right index finger down left
forearm and off elbow and
repeat.

fall (verb)

Right hand in V shape, palm in. Left hand open, palm up, fingers pointing out at an angle. Put tips of right V on left palm. Then turn right hand over quickly, ending with right V, palm up, on left palm.

family

Both hands in F shape, palms out, index fingers and thumbs touching. Move hands out in circle, ending with little fingers touching.

far

Both hands in 10 shape, palms facing, thumbs up, knuckles touching. Move right hand forward.

fast

Both index fingers extended, thumbs slightly up, palms facing. Hold left hand ahead of right hand in front of body. Then jerk hands back toward body while closing index fingers.

father

Right hand in 5 shape, palm facing left, fingers pointing up. Tap tip of thumb on center of forehead.

fault

Right hand open and bent. Place fingertips on right shoulder and tap once.

feel

Right hand in 5 shape, palm in, fingers pointing left. Place tip of bent middle finger on chest and move upward several times.

few

Right hand in A shape, palm up. Beginning with thumb, uncurl each finger slowly as hand moves slightly to right.

find, pick up

Right hand open in front of body, palm down, fingers pointing out. Close tips of thumb and index finger while lifting hand.

fine

Right hand in 5 shape, palm facing left. Place thumb on chest. Then move hand away from body.

fingerspelling

Right hand open in front of chest, palm down, fingers pointing out. Wiggle fingers while moving hand from left to right.

finish

Both hands in 5 shape in front of chest, palms in at an angle. Twist hands and lower slightly, ending with palms out at an angle.

fire

Both hands in 5 shape in front of chest, palms in, fingers pointing up. Wiggle fingers while moving hands up and down in alternate motions.

first

Right hand in ONE shape, palm facing left. Left hand in 10 shape, palm facing right. Strike inside of left thumb with inside of right index finger.

floor

Both hands in B shape, palms down, index fingers touching. Move hands apart to sides.

flower

Right hand in AND shape, palm in. First touch right side of nose with thumb and fingertips, then touch left side.

fly (verb)

Right thumb, index and little fingers extended, palm down. Move hand from near right shoulder forward and up.

follow

Both hands in 10 shape, thumbs up. Put right hand behind left hand. Then move hands forward at same time.

food, eat

Right hand in AND shape.
Touch lips with fingertips
several times.

for

Right hand in ONE shape,
palm in. Place fingertip on
right forehead. Then move
hand down and out, ending
with index finger pointing up
and palm out.

fork

Right hand in V shape,
fingers pointing down. Left
hand open, palm up, fingers
pointing out. Tap right V
fingertips against left palm
and repeat.

Friday

Right hand in F shape, palm in, fingers pointing up. Move hand in small circle.

friend

Both hands in ONE shape, right palm down, left palm up, index fingers bent. Hook right index finger over left index finger. Repeat in reverse hand positions.

from

Right hand in X shape, palm facing left. Left hand in ONE shape, palm out, index finger pointing up. Place knuckle of right index finger against back of left index finger. Then pull right hand toward body.

full

Right hand open, palm down, fingers pointing out at an angle. Left hand in S shape, palm facing right. Brush right palm to left across left index finger and thumb.

fun

Both hands in H shape, right palm facing left, left palm down. Brush right H fingertips against right side of nose. Then move right hand out and down onto left H.

future, will (verb)

Right hand open, palm facing left, fingers pointing up. Hold hand at right side of face. Then move hand out, ending with fingers pointing out.

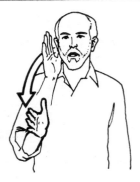

Gg

game

Both hands in 10 shape in front of chest, palms in, knuckles facing. Move hands together, ending with knuckles touching.

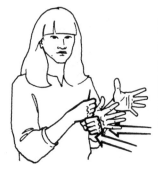

get, obtain, receive

Both hands in 5 shape, palms facing, fingers pointing out. Draw hands toward body while closing both to S shape, ending with right hand on left hand.

girl

Right hand in A shape, palm facing left. Place hand against right cheek. Then draw thumb tip down cheek to jaw.

give

Both hands in AND shape, palms up, close to chest. Move hands forward and out.

glass

Right hand in C shape, palm facing left. Left hand open, palm up, fingers pointing right. Put edge of right little finger on left palm. Then raise right hand up slightly.

glasses

Both hands with curved thumbs and index fingers, other fingers closed, palms facing. Put hands near eyes on either side of face. Then tap cheeks twice with thumbs.

go

Both hands in ONE shape, palms out, index fingers pointing up. Hold right hand closer to body. Then, by flicking the wrists, move index fingers down, ending with index fingers pointing out.

God

Right hand open, palm facing left, fingers pointing up. Hold hand out from and above head. Then bring hand inward and down toward face in an arc.

good

Right hand open, palm in, fingers pointing up. Left hand open, palm up. Place right fingertips on lips. Then move hand down and away from mouth, ending with palm up inside left palm.

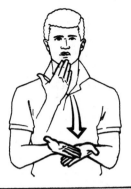

good-bye

Right hand open, palm out. Move hand back and forth in waving motion.

grab, take

Right hand in curved 5 shape at right side of body, palm down, fingers out. Move hand up to chest while closing to S shape.

grass

Right hand open and slightly curved, palm up. Place heel of hand under chin and move up slightly twice.

green

Right hand in G shape in front of chest. Shake G several times.

grow

Right hand in AND shape, palm in, fingers pointing up. Left hand in C shape, palm in. While moving right hand up through left C, open right hand into 5 shape.

hair

Right hand in O shape. Hold
a little hair between thumb
and index finger and shake.

hands

Both hands B shape, palms
in. Brush across little finger
side of left hand with index
finger side of right hand.
Then reverse.

happy

Right hand open, palm in, fingers pointing left. Pat chest with upward movement several times.

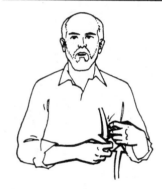

hard (difficult), difficult

Both hands in bent V shape, palms in. Move hands up and down alternately, striking knuckles together as they pass.

hard (substance)

Both hands in bent V shape. Strike side of left hand with side of right hand.

have (possess)

Both hands open and bent, palms facing chest, fingers pointing in. Move hands in and place fingertips on chest.

he, her, him, it, she

Right hand in ONE shape, palm down. Point outward with index finger in the direction of the person being referred to.

head

Right hand open and bent, palm facing left. First touch right temple with fingertips, and then move hand down and touch right cheek.

hear

Right hand in ONE shape. Put index fingertip at right ear.

heart

Right hand in 5 shape, palm in, middle finger bent. Touch chest in area of heart with middle fingertip twice.

help, assist

Left hand open, palm up. Right hand in 10 shape, palm in, resting on left palm. Raise right hand with left hand.

her, he, him, it, she

Right hand in ONE shape,
palm down. Point outward
with index finger in the
direction of the person being
referred to.

here

Both hands in 5 shape in
front of waist, palms up,
fingers pointing out. Move
hands side to side in
opposite directions and
repeat.

hers, his, its

Right hand open, palm out,
fingers pointing up. Hold
hand out at right side of
body, chest high, and move
forward slightly in the
direction of the person being
referred to.

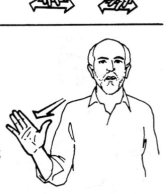

highway

Both hands in H shape, right hand near right shoulder, palm out, left hand in front of left shoulder, palm in. Move right hand outward while moving left hand inward and repeat.

him, he, her, it, she

Right hand in ONE shape, palm down. Point outward with index finger in the direction of the person being referred to.

hire, invite, welcome

Right hand open and curved, palm in. Bring hand from front of body in toward waist.

his, hers, its

Right hand open, palm out,
fingers pointing up. Hold
hand out at right side of
body, chest high, and move
forward slightly in the
direction of the person being
referred to.

hold

Both hands in S shape in
front of chest, palms in.
Place little finger side of right
hand on index finger side of
left hand. Then bring hands
in slightly toward chest.

holiday, vacation

Both hands in 5 shape,
palms in at an angle. Tap
thumbs beneath shoulders
twice.

home

Right hand in AND shape. Place fingertips on lower cheek, and then move them to upper cheek.

hot

Right hand in curved 5 shape, palm in, fingers pointing up. Put hand near mouth. Then twist hand out and down, ending with palm down.

hour

Right hand in ONE shape, index finger pointing up. Left hand open, fingers pointing out. Place right knuckles on left palm. Then move right index finger in a clockwise motion around left palm, ending with index finger in original position.

house

Both hands open in front of
face, palms down at an
angle, fingertips touching.
Draw hands apart and down
at an angle to sides of body.
Then move hands straight
down with palms facing.

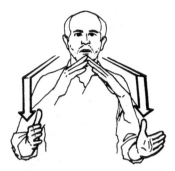

how

Both hands in 10 shape,
palms in, knuckles
touching. Turn hands up,
ending with palms up.

hungry

Right hand in C shape, palm
in. Put fingertips near throat
and move hand down the
chest.

hurry

Both hands in H shape, palms facing, fingers pointing out. Move hands forward alternately in quick up-and-down movements.

hurt, ache

Both hands in ONE shape, palms in, right index finger pointing left, left index finger pointing right. With hands in front of chest, move index fingers toward each other several times without touching.

husband

Right hand in open and bent shape, thumb extended and bent, touching right side of head. Left hand open in front of body, palm up, fingers pointing right. Move right hand down and clasp left hand.

I i

I, me

Right hand in ONE shape.
Point finger at center of
chest.

ice cream

Right hand in S shape, palm
facing left. Hold hand in
front of mouth and move it
down several times as if
licking an ice cream cone.

idea

Right hand in I shape, palm in. Touch little fingertip to forehead. Then move hand out and slightly up.

ill, sick

Both hands in 5 shape, palms in, middle fingers bent. Touch forehead with right middle fingertip while touching stomach with left middle fingertip.

important, valuable

Both hands in F shape side by side in front of waist, palms up. Move hands up and around, ending with palms down, thumbs touching.

in

Right hand in AND shape,
palm in, fingers pointing
down. Left hand in C shape,
palm facing right. Put right
fingertips into left C.

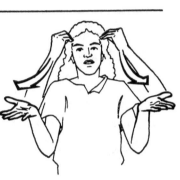

inform,
information, notify

Both hands in AND shape,
palms in. Place hands at
forehead. Then move hands
down and out, ending with
hands open, palms up.

inside

Right hand in AND shape,
palm in, fingers pointing
down. Left hand in C shape,
palm facing right. Put right
fingertips into left C and
repeat.

interesting

Both hands in 5 shape, palms in. Bend middle fingers and thumbs and place tips on chest with right hand above left hand. Draw hands away from body while closing tips of middle fingers and thumbs.

introduce

Both hands open at sides of body, palms up, fingers facing. Bring hands toward each other, ending with fingertips touching.

invite, hire, welcome

Right hand open and curved, palm in. Bring hand from front of body in toward waist.

is (all forms of *be*)

Right hand in ONE shape, palm facing left. Place index fingertip at lips. Then move finger out in short, straight line. (Note: This sign can be initialized using the I shape.)

it, he, her, him, she

Right hand in ONE shape, palm down. Point outward with index finger in the direction of the object being referred to.

its, hers, his

Right hand open, palm out, fingers pointing up. Hold hand out at right side of body, chest high, and move forward slightly in the direction of the object being referred to.

J j

job, work

Both hands in S shape, palms facing at an angle. Tap left hand with heel of right hand several times.

judge (verb)

Both hands in F shape in front of body, palms facing, fingers pointing out. Raise and lower hands in short, alternate movements.

K k

keep

Both hands in K shape, right palm facing left, left palm facing right. Tap little finger side of right hand against index finger side of left hand twice.

key

Right hand in X shape, palm down. Left hand open, palm facing right, fingers pointing out. Place knuckle of right index finger on left palm and twist.

kind (type)

Both hands in K shape, fingers pointing out. Place little finger side of right hand on index finger side of left hand. Then circle right hand out and around left hand, ending with right hand on left hand.

knife

Both hands in ONE shape. Slide right index finger along left index finger several times.

know

Right hand open and slightly bent, fingers pointing in. Touch forehead with fingertips.

large, big

Both hands in curved L shape in front of chest, palms in at an angle. Move hands out, ending with palms facing out.

last

Both hands in I shape, right palm facing left, left palm in. Hold right hand above left hand. Then move right hand down, striking left little finger with right little finger.

late, yet

Right hand open near waist, palm facing back, fingers pointing down. Move hand back and forth several times.

later

Right hand in L shape, palm out. Left hand open, palm facing right, fingers pointing up. Place right thumb on left palm with index finger pointing up. Then twist right hand down, ending with index finger pointing out.

law

Right hand in L shape. Left hand open, palm out. Place right knuckles on left palm first at fingers and then at heel.

lead (verb)

Right hand in flat C shape.
Left hand open, palm in,
fingers pointing right. Grasp
left fingertips between right
thumb and fingertips and
pull left hand to right.

learn

Right hand in curved 5 shape,
palm down. Left hand open,
palm up. Place right fingertips on left palm. Then bring
right hand up toward
forehead while closing to
AND shape.

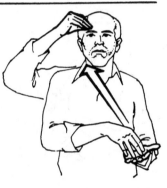

leave

Both hands open in front of
body, palms down. Draw
hands toward right shoulder
while closing to A shape.

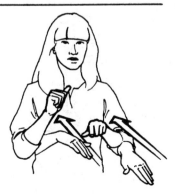

left (direction)

Right hand in L shape, palm out, index finger pointing up. Move hand from right to left in front of body.

let, allow, way

Both hands open in front of waist, palms facing, fingers pointing out. Move hands out and slightly up.

letter

Right hand in 10 shape, palm in. Left hand open in front of chest, palm at an angle facing right, fingers pointing out. Touch lips with right thunb. Then move right hand down and place right thumb on left palm.

library

Right hand in L shape, palm out. Make clockwise circle with right hand.

life, live

Both hands in L shape in front of waist, palms in, index fingers pointing toward each other. Move hands up, ending with hands in front of chest.

light, bright, clear

Both hands in AND shape in front of chest, palms out. Move hands up and away from each other, opening to 5 shape, palms out.

like (verb)

Right hand in 5 shape, palm in, thumb and middle finger bent. Place tips of thumb and middle finger on chest. Draw hand away from body while closing tips of thumb and middle finger.

listen

Right hand in C shape, palm out. Place C against right ear.

little (height), short (height), small (height)

Right hand open at right side. Bounce hand down slightly.

little (size), small (size)

Both hands open in front of chest, palms facing, fingers pointing out. Move hands a short distance toward each other and repeat.

live, life

Both hands in L shape in front of waist, palms in, index fingers pointing toward each other. Move hands up, ending with hands in front of chest.

loan

Both hands in K shape in front of upper chest, fingers pointing up. Put little finger side or right K hand on index finger side of left K hand. Then move hands up and out, ending with fingers pointing out.

lock

Both hands in S shape, right palm out, left palm down. Hold right hand above left hand. Circle and twist right hand firmly, ending with back of right hand on back of left hand.

long

Right hand in ONE shape, palm down. Left arm extended out and slightly down, palm down. Draw right index finger up left arm.

look

Right hand in V shape in front of face, palm down, fingers pointing out. Move hand outward.

lose, lost

Both hands in AND shape,
palms in, fingertips touching.
Move hands down and apart,
ending with hands in 5
shape, palms down.

love

Both hands in A shape,
palms in. Place hands
crossed at wrists on chest.

lunch

Right hand in L shape near
right side of mouth, palm
left. Move hand in, touching
face with tip of thumb twice.

Mm

machine

Both hands in curved 5 shape in front of chest, palms in, thumbs up. Mesh fingers of two hands loosely. Then move hands up and down from wrists several times.

mad, angry

Right hand in 5 shape, palm in, fingers pointing up. Place hand in front of face. Then bend fingers, ending in CLAW shape.

make

Both hands in S shape, palms facing in. Place little finger side of right hand on index finger side of left hand. Twist hands in opposite directions.

man

Right hand in A shape, palm facing left. Put thumb on forehead. Then draw hand away and down, opening hand and ending with thumb on chest and fingers pointing out.

manage, control, direct

Both hands in X shape in front of chest, palms facing, knuckles pointing out. Move hands in and out alternately.

many

Both hands in S shape in front of chest, palms up. Open and close hands quickly several times.

maybe

Both hands open, palms up, fingers pointing out. Move hands up and down alternately.

me, I

Right hand in ONE shape. Point finger at center of chest.

meat

Right hand in 5 shape. Left hand open, palm in, fingers pointing right. Grasp left hand between thumb and index finger with right thumb and index finger.

medicine

Right hand in 5 shape, palm down, middle finger bent. Left hand open, palm up. Rub right middle fingertip in left palm.

meet

Both hands in ONE shape at sides, palms facing, index fingers pointing up. Move hands toward each other in front of chest until they meet.

meeting

Both hands in curved 5 shape in front of chest, palms facing. Bring hands together, closing to AND shape with fingertips touching. Then move hands apart while opening them, and repeat.

milk

Right hand in S shape in front of body, palm facing left. Open and close hand in squeezing motion several times.

mine, my

Right hand open, palm in, fingers pointing left. Place palm on chest.

minute

Right hand in ONE shape, index finger pointing up. Left hand open, fingers pointing up at an angle. Place right knuckles on left palm. Then twist right hand slightly, moving index finger forward.

miss (fail)

Right hand open, palm facing left, near right side of face. Move hand in an arc across the face, closing to S shape.

miss (feel lack of), disappoint

Right hand in ONE shape, palm in. Touch chin with index fingertip.

mistake, wrong

Right hand in Y shape, palm in. Touch chin twice with knuckles of right closed fingers.

Monday

Right hand in M shape, palm in. Move hand in small circle.

money

Right hand in AND shape, palm up. Left hand open, palm up. Tap back of right hand on left palm several times.

month

Both hands in ONE shape, right palm in, index finger pointing left; left palm facing right, index finger pointing up. Move right index finger down side of left index finger from tip to base.

more

Both hands in AND shape, palms in, fingers pointing toward each other. Tap fingertips together.

morning

Both hands open, right palm up, left palm in. Put fingertips of left hand in crook of slightly bent, extended right arm. Then move right hand up toward face.

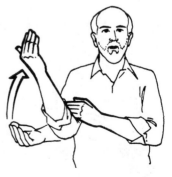

mother

Right hand in 5 shape, palm facing left. Tap tip of thumb on chin.

mouth

Right hand in ONE shape, palm in. Circle mouth with index finger.

move

Both hands in AND shape side by side in front of body, palms down. Move hands slightly forward and to right.

much

Both hands in CLAW shape, palms facing, fingertips almost touching and pointing out. Move hands apart.

must, have to, need

Right hand in X shape, palm down. Move X index finger down forcefully once.

my, mine

Right hand open, palm in, fingers pointing left. Place palm on chest.

Nn

name

Both hands in H shape, palms facing. Put right middle finger at an angle across left index finger and tap twice.

near

Both hands open, palms in, right fingers pointing left, left fingers pointing right. Place left hand in front of right hand. Then move back of right hand close to left palm.

necessary

Right hand in X shape, palm
down. Move X index finger
up and down forcefully
twice.

need, have to, must

Right hand in X shape, palm
down. Move X index finger
down forcefully once.

never

Right hand in B shape at
right side of head, palm left,
fingers pointing up. Move
hand around and down to
waist, ending with palm
down, fingers pointing out.

new

Both hands open, palms up. Brush back of right hand across left palm from right to left.

newspaper, print

Right hand in G shape, palm down, thumb and index finger pointing out. Left hand open, palm up, fingers pointing out. Close and open right thumb and index finger on the left palm several times.

next

Both hands open, palms in, right fingers pointing left, left fingers pointing right. Place left hand in front of right hand. Then move right hand up and over left hand.

nice, clean

Both hands open, right palm down, left palm up. Place right palm on heel of left palm. Then move right hand across to left fingertips.

night

Right hand open and bent, palm down, fingers pointing out. Left hand open and curved palm down, fingers pointing right. Tap right wrist against back of left hand.

no

Right thumb, index and middle fingers extended, palm out. Bring three tips together in a quick movement.

noise

Right hand in ONE shape. Point to right ear. Then, with both hands in 5 shape, palms down, move hands out and shake them side to side.

none

Both hands in O shape side by side in front of body, palms out. Move hands away from each other to sides.

noon

Right hand open, palm facing left, fingers pointing up. Left hand open, palm down, fingers pointing right. Put right elbow on back of left hand.

nose

Right hand in ONE shape,
palm in. Touch nose with
fingertip.

not, don't

Right hand in 10 shape,
palm facing left. Put tip of
thumb under chin and move
hand outward.

nothing

Right hand in S shape under
chin, palm facing left. Move
hand down and outward,
ending with hand open,
palm down, fingers pointing
out.

notify, inform, information

Both hands in AND shape, palms in. Place hands at forehead. Then move hands down and out, ending with hands open, palms up.

now

Both hands in Y shape in front of body, palms up. Drop hands at same time.

number

Both hands in AND shape, palms facing, fingertips touching. Twist hands in opposite directions.

Oo

obtain, get, receive

Both hands in 5 shape, palms facing, fingers pointing out. Draw hands toward body while closing both to S shape, ending with right hand on left hand.

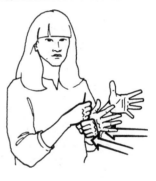

offer

Both hands open in front of upper chest, palms in, fingers pointing up at an angle. Move hands down and outward in curved motion, ending with palms up, fingers pointing out.

office

Both hands in O shape in front of body, palms down. Put left hand in front of right hand. Then move hands to sides of body.

often

Right hand open and bent. Left hand open, palm up, fingers pointing out. Touch right fingertips against left palm and repeat.

old

Right hand in C shape, palm facing left. Place hand at chin. Then move hand out and down closing to S shape.

on

Both hands open, palms down, right fingers pointing left, left fingers pointing out. Place right palm on back of left hand.

open

Both hands in B shape side by side, palms down. Move hands apart and up, ending with palms up.

or, either, then

Right hand in ONE shape. Left hand in L shape, palm facing right, index finger pointing out. With right index finger, first touch left thumb, then left index finger.

orange

Right hand in S shape. Open and close hand in squeezing motion two or three times in front of mouth.

other, another

Right hand in 10 shape, palm down. Move hand up and to right, ending with palm up.

our, ours

Right hand open, palm facing left, fingers pointing up. Place thumb side of hand at right shoulder. Then circle hand out and around, ending with little finger side of hand at left shoulder.

out

Right hand open, fingers
pointing down. Left hand in
C shape, palm facing right.
Put right hand inside left C
hand. Then draw right hand
up and out, closing it to
AND shape.

outside

Right hand open, fingers
pointing down. Left hand in
C shape, palm facing right.
Put right hand inside left C
hand. Then draw right hand
up and out, closing it to
AND shape and repeat.

over, above

Both hands open, palms
down, right fingers pointing
left, left fingers pointing
right. Place right palm on
back of left hand. Move right
hand up away from body
and then around and toward
body.

P p

pants

Both hands open and bent at sides, palms in, fingertips on upper legs. Move hands up to waist.

paper

Both hands open, right palm down, left palm up, fingers pointing out at an angle. Brush heel of right hand across heel of left hand twice.

parents

Right hand in P shape, palm in. First touch forehead with middle fingertip, then touch chin.

parents

Right hand in 5 shape, palm left, fingers pointing out, thumb touching chin. Move hand up and touch forehead above right eye with tip of thumb. (Note: This sign can also be done by touching forehead first, then chin.)

park, parking

Right hand in 3 shape, palm facing left, fingers pointing out. Left hand open, palm up, fingers pointing out. Tap little finger side of right hand on left palm.

part

Both hands open, right palm facing left, left palm up. Draw little finger edge of right hand across left palm in toward body.

party

Both hands in P shape in front of body, palms facing. Swing hands from side to side two or three times.

pay

Right hand in ONE shape, palm down. Left hand open, palm up, fingers pointing out. Place right index fingertip on heel of left palm and slide it out across left fingers, ending with right index finger pointing out.

people

Both hands in P shape,
palms down. Alternately
circle hands outward in front
of body.

person

Both hands in P shape,
palms down. Place hands in
parallel position in front of
body. Then move hands
down at same time.

photograph, picture

Right hand in C shape, palm
out. Left hand open, palm
facing right, fingers pointing
up. Place right C at right
temple. Then move right
hand down, ending with
thumb and index finger of
right C against left palm.

pick, choose, select

Bend thumb and index finger of open right hand in front of chest, palm out. Then draw hand back while closing tips of thumb and index finger.

pick up, find

Right hand open in front of body, palm down, fingers pointing out. Close tips of thumb and index finger while lifting hand.

place

Both hands in P shape, palms facing, middle fingertips touching. Circle hands around and in toward body, ending with middle fingertips touching again.

plan (verb), arrange, schedule (verb)

Both hands open in front of body, palms facing, fingers pointing out. Move hands to right.

plate

Both hands in curved L shape, palms facing. Hold hands apart to show size of plate.

play (verb)

Both hands in Y shape, palms in. Twist hands back and forth several times.

please

Right hand open, palm in.
Rub right palm in circular
motion on chest.

police

Right hand in C shape, palm
facing left. Put thumb and
index finger edge of right C
against body just below left
shoulder.

practice

Right hand in A shape. Left
hand in ONE shape, palm
in, index finger pointing
right. Rub knuckles of right A
back and forth on left index
finger twice.

prefer, rather

Right hand open on chest, palm in, fingers pointing left. Move hand slightly up and to right while closing to 10 shape.

president

Both hands open, palms out. Put hands at sides of forehead. Move hands out to sides while closing to S shape.

pretty

Right hand in 5 shape near chin, palm in, fingers pointing up. Move hand in circle in front of face while closing to AND shape, ending near chin.

price

Right hand in X shape, palm in. Left hand open, palm facing right, fingers pointing out. Move right bent index finger down left palm twice.

print, newspaper

Right hand in G shape, palm down, thumb and index finger pointing out. Left hand open, palm up, fingers pointing out. Close and open right thumb and index finger on the left palm several times.

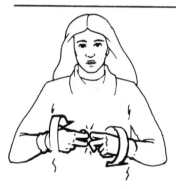

problem

Both hands in bent U shape, palms in, knuckles of index and middle fingers facing and touching. Twist wrists to rub knuckles against each other.

program

Right hand in P shape. Left
hand open, palm in, fingers
pointing up. Move right
middle fingertip up left palm
from heel to tips. Then move
right P down back of left
hand.

project

Right hand in P shape. Left
hand open, palm in, fingers
pointing up. Move right
middle fingertip up left palm
from heel to tips. Then
change right hand to J shape
and move right J down back
of left hand.

promise

Right hand in ONE shape,
palm facing left, index finger
pointing up. Left hand in S
shape, palm facing right. Put
right index finger at mouth.
Then move hand down while
opening it, ending with open
right hand on side of left S
hand.

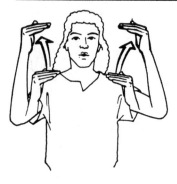

promotion

Both hands open and bent, palms down, fingertips pointing toward each other. Move hands up at same time.

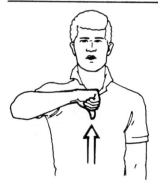

proud

Right hand in A shape, thumb pointing down. Place thumbnail against lower chest and move thumb up.

put

Both hands in AND shape side by side in front of body, palms down. Move hands outward in an arc.

Qq

question

Right hand in ONE shape, palm out, index finger pointing up. Draw a question mark with right index finger, ending with finger pointing out.

quiet

Both hands in B shape, palms facing, fingers pointing out at an angle. Put hands at mouth, left hand in front of right hand. Then move hands down and apart, ending with palms down.

R r

radio

Right hand in C shape. Put hand over right ear and tap twice. (Note: Can also be done using both hands in the C shape.)

rain

Both hands in 5 shape, palms out. Hold hands in front of body at shoulder level. Drop hands a short distance and repeat.

rather, prefer

Right hand open on chest, palm in, fingers pointing left. Move hand slightly up and to right while closing to 10 shape.

read

Right hand in V shape, palm down. Left hand open, palm up, fingers pointing out. Place right V fingertips on left fingertips. Then move right V down and up left palm.

ready

Both hands in R shape, palms down, R fingers pointing left. Move both hands to right.

real, true

Right hand in ONE shape in front of lips, palm facing left, index finger pointing up. Touch lips with index fingertip. Then move hand out, ending with index finger pointing out.

really, sure

Right hand in ONE shape, palm facing left. Touch lips with index fingertip. Then move finger up and out in an arc.

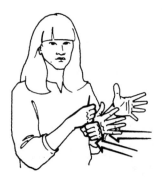

receive, get, obtain

Both hands in 5 shape, palms facing, fingers pointing out. Draw hands toward body while closing both to S shape, ending with right hand on left hand.

red

Right hand in ONE shape, palm in, index finger pointing up. Draw index fingertip down and across lips twice.

remember

Both hands in A shape; right thumb on right side of forehead, left hand in front of chest. Move right hand down and touch left thumbnail with right thumb.

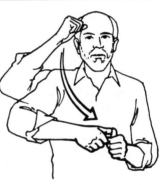

reservation

Both hands in S shape, right palm facing left, left palm down. Move right hand out and down on top of left hand.

responsibility

Both hands in R shape, palms down. Place both hands on right shoulder. Then tap shoulder twice with tips of R fingers.

rest

Both hands open, palms in. Cross arms and lay palms of hands near shoulders.

restroom

Right hand in R shape, palm down, R fingers pointing out. Bounce hand down and then to right.

right (correct), correct (adjective)

Both hands in ONE shape, palms facing, index fingers pointing out. Strike edge of right little finger on top of left index finger.

right (direction)

Right hand in R shape in front of left shoulder, palm out, R fingers pointing up. Move hand out to right.

ring (noun)

Both hands open, palms in. Place tips of right thumb and index finger on either side of base of left ring (4th) finger. Then move right thumb and index finger back and forth on ring finger.

road, street

Both hands open, palms facing, fingers pointing out. Hold hands a few inches apart in front of waist. Then move hands forward.

room

Both hands in R shape in front of body, palms in, right fingers pointing left, left fingers pointing right. Place left hand in front of right hand. Then move hands to sides, ending with palms facing each other and R fingers pointing out.

run (physical activity)

Both hands in L shape, palms facing, index fingers pointing out. Hook right index finger around left thumb. Bend both index fingers and thumbs several times while moving hands forward.

salt

Both hands in V shape, palms down. Tap right index and middle fingers alternately on back of left V index and middle fingers several times.

same

Both hands in ONE shape at sides, palms down, index fingers pointing out. Move hands together, ending with sides of index fingers touching.

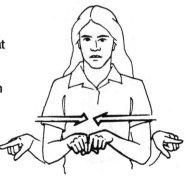

same

Right hand in Y shape in front of chest, palm down. Move hand from side to side.

Saturday

Right hand in S shape, palm in. Move hand in small circle.

save (money)

Right hand in V shape, palm in. Left hand in S shape, palm facing right. Tap right V fingers against side of left hand.

say

Right hand in ONE shape, palm in, index finger pointing left. Move index finger up and out in an arc in front of mouth twice.

schedule (noun)

Both hands in 5 shape, right palm out, fingers pointing up; left palm in, fingers pointing right. Move right fingertips down left palm. Then turn right hand over and move the back of right fingertips across left palm from heel to fingertips.

schedule (verb), arrange, plan (verb)

Both hands open in front of body, palms facing, fingers pointing out. Move hands to right.

school

Both hands open, right palm down, fingers pointing out; left palm up, fingers pointing right. Clap hands twice.

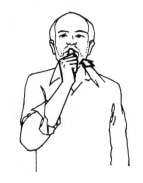

secret

Right hand in A shape, palm facing left. Tap right thumbnail against lips twice.

secretary

Right hand in K shape, palm facing left. Left hand open, palm up, fingers pointing right. Put tips of right K fingers at mouth. Then bring right hand down, and move right K fingers along left palm.

see

Right hand in V shape, palm in, V fingers pointing up. Put tips of V fingers in front of eyes. Then move hand out away from eyes.

seem

Right hand open and curved, palm out, fingers pointing up. Hold hand at side near right shoulder. Then turn hand so palm faces body.

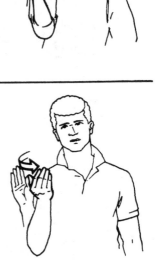

select, choose, pick

Bend thumb and index finger of open right hand in front of chest, palm out. Then draw hand back while closing tips of thumb and index finger.

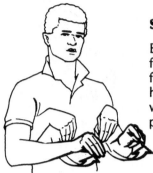

sell

Both hands in AND shape in front of chest, palms in, fingers pointing down. Move hands up and out by flicking wrists, ending with fingers pointing out.

send

Both hands open, palms down, right hand bent. Place right fingertips on back of left hand. Then flick right fingertips up and out.

send

Right hand in O shape near right shoulder, palm out. Move hand outward, ending with hand open, palm down, fingers pointing out.

she, he, her, him, it

Right hand in ONE shape, palm down. Point outward with index finger in the direction of the person being referred to.

shirt

Both thumbs and index fingers extended and touching, other fingers closed, near shoulders, palms in. Grasp clothes between thumbs and index fingers and pull out slightly.

shoes

Both hands in S shape in front of waist, palms down. Hit thumb sides of hands together twice.

short (height), little (height), small (height)

Right hand open at right side. Bounce hand down slightly.

short (length), soon

Both hands in H shape, palms facing at an angle. Put right H across left H and move right fingers back and forth on left fingers.

show (verb), example

Right hand in ONE shape, palm in. Left hand open, palm out, fingers pointing up. Place right index fingertip on left palm. Then move both hands forward.

sick, ill

Both hands in 5 shape, palms in, middle fingers bent. Touch forehead with right middle fingertip while touching stomach with left middle fingertip.

sign (language)

Both hands in ONE shape, palms facing. Move hands outward in alternating circles by moving arms.

sister

Left hand in L shape in front of waist, thumb up, index finger pointing out. Place right hand in 10 shape on right cheek. Then bring right hand down while changing to L shape, ending with right hand resting on left hand.

sit

Right hand in bent V shape, palm down. Left hand in H shape in front of lower chest, palm down. Place right V fingers across left H fingers.

skirt

Both hands in 5 shape, palms in, fingers pointing down. Put hands at sides of waist and brush them down and slightly out.

sleep

Right hand in 5 shape, palm in, fingers pointing up. Place hand in front of face. Then move it down near chin while closing hand to AND shape.

slow

Both hands open, palms down, fingers pointing out. Place right fingers on back of left hand and draw right hand up left arm.

small (height), little (height), short (height)

Right hand open at right side. Bounce hand down slightly.

small (size), little (size)

Both hands open at sides of body, palms facing, fingers pointing out. Move hands a short distance toward each other and repeat.

smell

Right hand open, palm up, fingers pointing left. Put palm in front of nose and move it up slightly two or three times.

smoke

Right hand in V shape at lips, palm in, V fingers pointing up. Move V fingers out from lips a short distance and repeat.

snow

Both hands in 5 shape above shoulders, palms down. Move hands down while wiggling fingers.

socks

Both hands in ONE shape, palms down, index fingers pointing out. Place index fingers side by side. Then rub them in and out alternately several times.

soda

Right hand in 5 shape, palm down. Left hand in S shape, palm in. Put right middle finger into left S hand. Immediately raise right hand up and then slap side of left S with right palm.

soft

Both hands in curved 5 shape in front of body, palms and fingers up. Drop hands down while closing to AND shape, opening and closing fingertips several times.

some

Both hands open, right palm facing left, left palm up. Draw little finger edge of right hand across left palm in toward body.

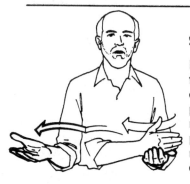

something

Both hands open, right palm facing left, fingers pointing out; left palm up, fingers pointing right. Draw edge of right little finger across left palm in toward body. Then move right hand out to right, ending with palm up.

son

Right hand in B shape, palm out. Left arm bent with left hand in front of waist, palm up. Put right index finger against forehead. Then move right hand down to crook of left arm, ending with palm up.

soon, short (length)

Both hands in H shape, palms facing at an angle. Put right H across left H and move right fingers back and forth on left fingers.

sorry

Right hand in A shape, palm in. Rub hand in a circular motion over heart several times.

spoon

Right hand in H shape, palm up. Left hand open in front of chest, palm up, fingers pointing out. Move tips of right H fingers across left palm in scooping motion up to mouth and repeat.

spring (season)

Right hand in AND shape, palm in, fingers pointing up. Left hand in C shape, palm in. While moving right hand up through left C, open right hand into 5 shape and repeat.

stand

Right hand in V shape, palm in, V fingers pointing down. Left hand open in front of chest, palm up. Put tips of right V fingers on left palm.

start, begin

Right hand in ONE shape, palm down, index finger pointing left. Left hand in 5 shape, palm facing right, fingers pointing out. Twist right index finger between left index and middle fingers.

stay

Both hands in Y shape in front of chest, palms down, thumbs touching. Move right hand out and down a little.

stop

Both hands open, right palm facing left, fingers pointing out; left palm up, fingers pointing right at an angle. In a forceful motion, move right hand down on left palm.

store

Both hands in AND shape in front of chest, palms in, fingers pointing down. Move hands outward slightly in rocking motion twice, ending with palms down, fingers pointing out.

street, road

Both hands open, palms facing, fingers pointing out. Hold hands a few inches apart in front of waist. Then move hands forward.

student

Right hand in curved 5 shape, palm down. Left hand open, palm up, fingers pointing out. Place right fingertips on left palm. Lift right hand and move it to forehead while closing to AND shape. Then with both hands open at sides, palms facing, lower hands.

sugar, cute

Right hand in H shape, thumb extended, palm in. Place tips of index and middle fingers on chin. Brush chin several times with fingertips, ending with hand in 10 shape below chin.

summer

Right hand in ONE shape,
palm down, index finger
pointing left. Draw edge of
index finger across forehead
left to right while changing
to X shape.

sun

Right hand in C shape, palm
out. Tap right temple twice
with edge of right index
finger.

Sunday

Both hands in 5 shape in
front of chest, palms out,
fingers pointing up. Move
hands down slightly once.

supervise

Both hands in K shape, right palm facing left, left palm facing right. Put little finger side of right hand on index finger side of left hand. Then move hands in counter-clockwise motion.

suppose

Right hand in I shape, palm in. Tap little fingertip near right eye twice.

sweet

Right hand open, palm in, fingers pointing up. Brush chin with fingertips several times, ending with hand bent.

Tt

table, desk

Both hands open, palms
down, right fingers pointing
left, left fingers pointing
right. Move right forearm
and hand down and place
on top of left forearm and
hand; tap twice.

take, grab

Right hand in curved 5 shape
at right side of body, palm
down, fingers pointing out.
Move hand up to chest while
closing to S shape.

talk

Right hand in 5 shape, palm facing left, fingers pointing up. Tap edge of index finger against lips several times.

tall (object)

Right hand in ONE shape, palm out, index finger pointing up. Left hand open, palm facing right, fingers pointing up. Move edge of right index finger up left palm.

tall (person)

Right hand open at right side. Hold hand at shoulder level. Then move hand up several inches.

tea

Right hand in F shape, palm
down. Left hand in O shape,
fingers pointing right. Put
tips of right F fingers into left
O and repeat.

teach

Both hands in AND shape,
palms facing. Place hands at
sides of forehead. Move
them out from forehead,
then back to forehead and
out again.

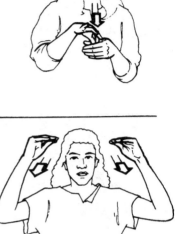

teacher

Both hands in AND shape,
palms facing. Place hands at
sides of forehead. Move
them out from forehead.
Then open hands, palms
facing, fingers pointing out.
Place hands in parallel
position in front of body and
move them down at same
time.

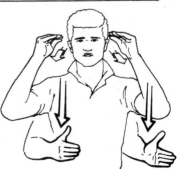

telephone

Right hand in Y shape. Put thumb near ear and little finger near mouth.

tell

Right hand in ONE shape, palm in. Put index fingertip on chin. Then move hand out, ending with index finger pointing up.

thank you

Right hand open, palm in, fingers pointing up. Put fingertips in front of mouth. Then move hand out and down, ending with palm up.

that

Right hand in Y shape, palm
down. Left hand open, palm
up, fingers pointing out.
Move right Y down onto left
palm.

their, theirs

Right hand open, palm out,
fingers pointing up. Hold
hand out at side. Then move
it to right.

them, they

Right hand in ONE shape,
palm facing right, index
finger pointing out. Move
finger to right.

then, either, or

Right hand in ONE shape.
Left hand in L shape, palm
facing right, index finger
pointing out. With right
index finger, first touch left
thumb, then left index finger.

they, them

Right hand in ONE shape,
palm facing right, index
finger pointing out. Move
finger to right.

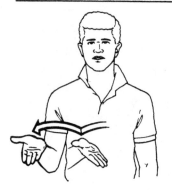

thing

Right hand open, palm up,
fingers pointing out. Hold
hand in front of body. Then
move hand to right in a
double movement.

think

Right hand in ONE shape.
Touch right temple with
index fingertip, palm down.

thirsty

Right hand in ONE shape,
palm in, index finger
pointing up. Move index
fingertip from upper to lower
part of throat.

this

Right hand in ONE shape,
palm down. Left hand open,
palm up, fingers pointing
out. Touch left palm with
right index fingertip.

through

Right hand open, palm facing left, fingers pointing out. Left hand open, palm in at an angle. Move right hand out between left index and middle fingers.

Thursday

Right hand in T shape, palm in. Change quickly to H shape in front of body.

ticket

Right hand in bent V shape. Left hand open, palm in, fingers pointing up. Grasp little finger edge of left palm between right bent V fingers. Then move right V fingers in and out on edge of left palm twice.

time, watch (noun)

Right hand in ONE shape, palm down, index finger bent. Left hand in A shape, palm down. Tap back of left wrist with right index fingertip and repeat.

tired

Both hands open and bent, palms in. Place fingertips on chest. Then drop hands down, ending with sides of little fingers resting on chest, palms up.

to

Both hands in ONE shape in front of body, right palm down, index finger pointing left; left palm facing right, index finger pointing up. Touch left index fingertip with right index fingertip.

today

Both hands in Y shape at sides of chest, palms up. Drop hands at same time to waist level.

tomorrow

Right hand in 10 shape, palm facing left, thumb up. Put tip of thumb at right side of chin and move it forward in an arc.

town, city

Both hands open in front of chest, palms facing at an angle, fingertips touching. Move hands apart and to the right, ending with fingertips touching.

travel, trip

Right hand in bent V shape
in front of chest, palm
down. Move hand forward
with a wavy movement.

trouble, worry

Both hands in B shape,
palms down. Begin with
right hand near forehead.
Move hand down in front of
face and toward left
shoulder. Then with left hand
near forehead, move it down
in front of face and toward
right shoulder. Repeat.

true, real

Right hand in ONE shape in
front of lips, palm facing left,
index finger pointing up.
Touch lips with index
fingertip. Then move hand
out, ending with index finger
pointing out.

try

Both hands in T shape in front of waist, palms facing. Twist hands out and up in an arc.

Tuesday

Right hand in T shape, palm in. Move hand in small circle.

TV (television)

Right hand in T shape, palm out. Quickly change to V shape.

Uu

under

Right hand in 10 shape, palm facing left, thumb up. Left hand open, palm down, fingers pointing right. Move right hand from near chest down and under left palm.

understand

Right hand in S shape, palm in. Put hand at right side of forehead. Then extend right index finger by flicking it up and out slightly.

up

Right hand in ONE shape, palm out, index finger pointing up. Move finger up.

us, we

Right hand in ONE shape, palm in. Move finger from right shoulder out and around to left shoulder.

use

Right hand in U shape, palm out, fingers pointing up. Left hand in S shape, palm down, knuckles pointing right. With heel of right hand against side of left hand, circle right U over back of left hand.

Vv

vacation, holiday

Both hands in 5 shape, palms in at an angle. Tap thumbs beneath shoulders twice.

valuable, important

Both hands in F shape side by side in front of waist, palms up. Move hands up and around, ending with palms down, thumbs touching.

very

Both hands in V shape, palms facing, fingers pointing up. Put V fingertips together. Then move fingers apart.

visit

Both hands in V shape, palms in, fingers pointing up. Circle hands outward alternately in front of chest.

vote

Right hand in F shape, palm down. Left hand in O shape, fingers pointing right. Put tips of right F fingers into left O.

wait

Both hands in 5 shape, palms up, fingers pointing out. Hold right hand a little nearer body than left hand. Wiggle fingers of both hands.

walk

Both hands open, palms down. Move hands forward in alternate up and down motions.

wall

Both hands in B shape, palms out, fingers pointing up. Put index fingers side by side. Then move hands apart.

want

Both hands in CLAW shape in front of waist, palms up. Pull hands toward body.

was (all forms of *be*)

Right hand in ONE shape, palm facing left. Place index fingertip at lips. Then move finger out in short, straight line. (Note: This sign can be initialized by using the W shape changing to S shape as hand moves around toward right cheek.)

wash

Both hands in A shape, right palm down, left palm up. With right hand on left hand, rub right knuckles across left knuckles several times.

watch (noun), time

Right hand in ONE shape, palm down, index finger bent. Left hand in A shape, palm down. Tap back of left wrist with right index fingertip and repeat.

watch (verb)

Both hands in V shape, palms down, V fingers pointing out. Move hands in and out in short motions.

water

Right hand in W shape, palm facing left, fingers pointing up. Tap chin with side of index finger several times.

way, allow, let

Both hands open in front of waist, palms facing, fingers pointing out. Move hands out and slightly up.

we, us

Right hand in ONE shape, palm in. Move finger from right shoulder out and around to left shoulder.

weather

Both hands in W shape,
palms facing, fingers
pointing up. Place hands
together, thumbs touching.
Then twist hands back and
forth alternately several
times.

Wednesday

Right hand in W shape, palm
in. Move hand in small
circle.

week

Right hand in ONE shape,
palm down. Left hand open,
palm up. Put knuckles of
right closed fingers on heel
of left palm. Then move right
hand along left palm and off
fingertips.

weekend

Right hand in ONE shape, palm down. Left hand open, palm up. Put knuckles of right closed fingers on heel of left palm. Move right hand along left palm to fingertips. Then open right hand and drop off end of left fingertips.

weigh, weight

Both hands in H shape, palms facing. Place right middle finger at an angle across left index finger. Rock right hand up and down on left H fingers.

welcome, hire, invite

Right hand open and curved, palm in. Bring hand from front of body in toward waist.

were (all forms of *be*)

Right hand in ONE shape, palm facing left. Place index fingertip at lips. Then move finger out in short, straight line. (Note: This sign can be initialized by using the W shape changing to R shape as hand moves around toward right cheek.)

wet

Both hands in 5 shape, palms in, fingers pointing up. Right hand at chin, left hand below left shoulder. Touch chin with right fingertips. Then move both hands down to waist while closing to AND shape, palms up. Tap tips of thumbs against fingertips twice.

what

Right hand in ONE shape. Left hand open, palm facing right, fingers pointing out at an angle. Draw right index fingertip down across left palm.

when

Both hands in ONE shape, right palm down, index finger pointing left; left palm in, index finger pointing out at an angle. Make circle with right index finger above left index finger. Then touch left index fingertip with right index fingertip.

where

Right hand in ONE shape, palm out, index finger pointing up. Shake index finger from side to side.

which

Both hands in 10 shape, palms facing, thumbs up. Move hands up and down alternately in front of chest.

white

Right hand in 5 shape, palm in, fingers pointing left. Place tips of thumb and fingers on chest. Then move hand out while closing to AND shape.

who

Right hand in ONE shape, palm in, index finger pointing toward mouth. Make circle around mouth with finger.

who

Right hand in L shape, palm facing left, index finger pointing up. Place tip of thumb on chin and bend index finger and wiggle it up and down several times.

why

Right hand open, palm in. Place fingertips near forehead. Then move hand down and out while changing to Y shape.

wife

Right hand in open and bent shape, thumb extended and bent, touching right side of chin, palm left. Left hand open in front of body, palm up, fingers pointing right. Move right hand down and clasp left hand.

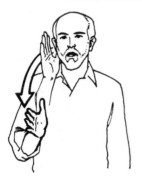

will (verb), future

Right hand open, palm facing left, fingers pointing up. Hold hand at right side of face. Then move hand out, ending with fingers pointing out.

win

Right hand in 5 shape at right shoulder level, palm facing left, fingers pointing up at an angle. Left hand in S shape in front of body, palm in. Close right hand to S shape while moving it down and across top of left hand.

wind (noun)

Both hands in 5 shape in front of chest, fingers pointing right, right palm out, left palm in. Move hands in semicircular movement to left, ending with fingers pointing left, right palm in, left palm out. Repeat several times.

window

Both hands in B shape, palms in, fingers pointing in opposite directions. Put little finger edge of right hand on index finger edge of left hand. Then move right hand up a short distance and repeat.

wine

Right hand in W shape, palm in, fingers pointing up. Rub W fingers in small circles on right cheek.

winter, cold

Both hands in S shape at sides, palms facing. Move hands back and forth toward each other in short, shaking motions.

wish

Right hand in C shape, palm in, fingertips on chest. Draw hand down center of chest.

with

Both hands in A shape a few inches apart in front of chest, palms facing. Bring hands together, knuckles touching.

woman

Right hand in A shape, palm facing left. Draw right thumb tip down right cheek and off the jaw, opening hand and ending with thumb on chest and fingers pointing out.

wonder (verb)

Right hand in ONE shape, palm in. Point index finger at right side of forehead and move in small circle.

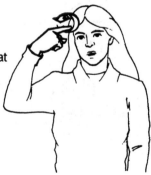

wonderful

Both hands in 5 shape, palms out, fingers pointing up. Hold hands at sides, above shoulders. Move hands out and in slightly twice.

word

Right hand in G shape, palm facing left, fingers pointing left. Left hand in ONE shape, palm facing right, index finger pointing up. Tap tips of right thumb and index finger against left index finger and repeat.

work, job

Both hands in S shape, palms facing at an angle. Tap left hand with heel of right hand several times.

worry, trouble

Both hands in B shape, palms down. Begin with right hand near forehead. Move hand down in front of face and toward left shoulder. Then with left hand near forehead, move it down in front of face and toward right shoulder. Repeat.

write

Right thumb and index finger extended, tips together, other fingers closed, palm down. Left hand open, palm up at an angle. Move tips of right thumb and index finger across left palm.

wrong, mistake

Right hand in Y shape, palm in. Touch chin twice with knuckles of right closed fingers.

X x

xerography

Right hand in X shape, palm facing left. Left hand open, palm down. Move right hand back and forth under left palm.

Y y

---

year

Both hands in S shape in front of body, palms facing. Hold right hand above left hand. Then circle right hand out and around left hand, ending with right hand on left hand.

---

yell

Right hand in CLAW shape, palm in. Place fingertips on sides of chin. Then move hand out and up.

yellow

Right hand in Y shape, palm out. Twist hand back and forth a few times.

yes

Right hand in S shape, palm out. Shake hand up and down by bending wrist and repeat.

yesterday

Right hand in A shape. Touch right side of chin with tip of right thumb. Then move tip of thumb back to right cheek. (Note: This sign can be initialized by using the right hand in the Y shape.)

yet, late

Right hand open near waist, palm facing back, fingers pointing down. Move hand back and forth several times.

you (singular)

Right hand in ONE shape. Point finger straight out.

you (plural)

Right hand in ONE shape. Point finger straight out and move it from left to right in front of body.

young

Both hands open and bent, palms in. Place fingertips at sides of upper chest. Then brush them up several times.

your, yours (singular)

Right hand open, palm out, fingers pointing up. Hold hand out in front of body.

your, yours (plural)

Right hand open, palm out, fingers pointing up. Hold hand out at left side of body and move it from left to right in front of body.

Zz

zipper

Both hands thumbs and index fingers touching, other fingers closed, palms in. Place right index finger on left index finger. Then move right hand up and down several times.

About Gallaudet and Sign Language

Gallaudet University is the foremost educational institution in the world for hearing-impaired people. The Gallaudet University Press is mandated to provide worthy materials related to the education of hearing-impaired people and those who work with them. This book is only one of a number of sign language and other books for and about the hearing-impaired community. If you would like to learn more sign language or more about deaf culture or deafness, please write or call us for our latest catalog.

Gallaudet University Press
800 Florida Avenue, NE
Washington, DC 20002
800-451-1073 (V/TDD)